# Lazarus
# & Object Pascal
# Notebook #4

978-1-312-67826-2

# Acknowledgement

To my new young friends, Mason, J.D. and Evelyn: May life and the good Lord fulfill your dreams, may you find much treasure and laughter, and may you make many good friends.

# Table of Contents

# Preface

I started this book using Python 3 but in the latest version of Ubuntu, which was 14.04, the default version of Python is 2.6, while this was easy to work around, I wondered if maybe I should check out the other "possible" languages on my list.

## Lazasrus & Object Pascal – I'm impressed

It meets all my favorite criteria. - It's open source – it's free of cost, it's multi-platform ( works on Windows, Linux and some Apples ). The IDE ( Integrated Development Environment ) does WYSIWYG ( What You See Is What You Get ) forms – and it does object code completion. The compiled & linked code is very fast, and the compile and link process is lightening quick.

# Why you want this book

-There are several, really good, tutorials on-line. But, **there comes a time when a programer just wants to see some example code. This book is filled with well tested, compiled and running code** not snippets. Where to define global variables, it's in here. where the semi-colons must be in an **If** or how to set up a Case statement, that's in here too. I'm no expert with Lazarus or Object Pascal, I'm a lowly student, just like you. I have been to a couple of the Internet forums where they entertain questions about Lazarus - a couple of times I even knew the answer, but alas, I couldn't respond because I didn't have the required level of ~~condescension~~ experience, to write an answer.

When I was younger, I had friends who used the Pascal language in their work, At that time I had started writing dBASE code, but I was curious and had bought a copy of Modula-2. Niklaus Wirth designed Pascal and Modula-2, so there were a number of similarities. Lazarus is very much like Borland's Delphi. Jenson & Partners spun out of Borland, and published my Modula-2 compiler. In fact, Anders Hejlsberg, earlier a Borland designer, also designed the C# language at Microsoft, as well as Delphi, at Borland. When it comes to programming, it's a smaller world than it seems.

The example for this book, is a simple desktop calculator. My entire source code listing is here. While Windows, Linux and the Mac come with calculators as part of the OS, making a new, simple calculator has became the subject of this book.

# I'll be using Lazarus 1.0.10 and Free Pascal (FPC) 2.6.2 32-bit.

There are newer and better versions of both language and IDE, but this version may be around for as many as five years. Ubuntu 14.04 is a LTS ( long term support ) version. So for now, I'll go with this version 1.0.10 of Lazarus and version 2.6.2 of Free Pascal ( FPC ). Since those are the default versions of the software in the Ubuntu software center with the newest version ( currently ) of the popular Ubuntu Linux.

## Conventions

In this book, the reader will notice that the source code is printed in a gray color with a bit of a gray background and a mono-spaced font. Text, where I am trying to say something, will appear in this handwriting font that I'm using right now.

## Pre-required knowledge for this book

The reader should have experience with some programming language on some computer. If you have experience with Pascal, all the better. There are many good language tutorials on the web, and many printed books are available from Amazon.com, BN.com, and other resources.

If you know another language other than Pascal, you should know that the colon and the equal symbol, together, are the required assignment characters. So X:=5; is how you would assign the numeric value 5 to the integer variable x. The other thing that you should know is that Pascal is context insensitive. Indents are important to make code human readable, but the compiler doesn't care. The semi-colon, is required to tell the language that the Pascal statement is complete. For example x:=5;  The semi-colon says to the compiler, "That statement is done".

Often, if I have a tip for you, I will put it in an indented block of Italicized text with a little cartoonish light-bulb in the left column like this:

*This is a tip*

*I would like to offer a word of thanks to Florian Paul Klämpfl ( the original author of Free Pascal ) and all those who have put their efforts into the Lazarus IDE and the Free Pascal compiler.*

# Chapter ½

Huh? How can I have a fractional chapter number? Well, I'm the author so it's a superpower that I have. The reason this chapter is here is that there are some programers that have a fair amount of experience, but haven't written a program like this – that has the graphical user interface built in. They won't do any exercises, or even read another chapter until they know it's worth it.

If this isn't for you, you can skip right on to chapter1 where I will try to explain how to build a desktop calculator. Often I will tell you why you might want to do a certain thing so you can use your new skills in future projects.

For you more advanced folks, here's a chapter with an example that is really simple to do and shows how easy it is to make a GUI program by barely trying. You don't even need to save this. It's a single form with a single button on it. Talk about simple!

Here we go:

1) Start Lazarus.

2) Create a new Application. From the main menu, pick Project/New Project/Application.

3) Bring focus to your new form by clicking on any of it, or clicking on the Toggle Form/Unit icon. This brings your form to the front.

4) Put a button on your form. Click on the button icon ( says "OK" on it ). Put it in the middle of your form and make the button about a third of an inch high, and about an inch wide.

5) The button should still be chosen. Find the property 'Caption' in the Object inspector. On the right side of the Object Inspector, change the value to 'GO'.

6) Highlight the *Events* tab of the 'GO' button, find the OnClick event ( 5 down from the top ). Double-Click in the value area. The made-up word 'Button1OnClick' appears and your cursor is sitting between the begin and end of a new handler procedure (  in the source editor window ) - created by Lazarus.

7) At the cursor's location, enter the single line of pascal code:

```
button1.Caption:='this is great';
```

The source code of the handler procedure looks like this now:

```
Procedure TForm1.Button1Click(Sender: TObject);
begin
  button1.Caption:='this is great';
end;
```

8) Now, compile, link & run your new program by pressing the green arrow. When the linking is complete, the form will come to the front. On your form, there is a single button that says GO on it, just like you designed it. When you click on the GO button, the caption on the button changes instantly to 'this is great'.

A new executable program called project1 (or project1.exe – in Windows) has been created and can be run like any other executable software program.

# Chapter 1

In this chapter, the reader will learn about the creation of a new form, how to change settings and how to save and reload your work. We will cover the basic design of the calculator form.

- Create a form
- Use the Object Inspector to change size and color and name of your form, even the form's Caption
- Where to put global variables
- How to save your work
- What's FormActivate for?

This project needs only one form. The body of the calculator. You can start this project by getting to the **Project** Menu at the top menu of Lazarus and pick "**Application**" from the menu that appears. A new, single form will be provided on the screen. The Lazarus IDE is very useful, it will **create the form** and put code in the associated Pascal unit source file to display and call the form. Lazarus is truly a RAD (Rapid Application Development) tool.

 *I check everything out on a very low powered Ubuntu machine just to be sure things work in a nearly worst case scenario ( I often develop on a speedy Windows PC ). When I tried to access the Top Lazarus main menu, I couldn't. I found that if I highlight the "Additional" tab then I can see and highlight and click one top level menu choice, like Project, then New. To get to the menu again, I click on the "Standard" tab. So, in other words, I simply click on any un-chosen tab then the top menu becomes available. No problem on the Windows machine.*

Before you really get started, you might want to draw your form on paper. In fact, if I were writing this for a customer, I would draw out the form and jot down the way the form would work. If the customer wanted more features, they would usually know that the price was going up, to cover the cost of the new features. There was very little confusion about the price of the end product. The form's rules of operation, often became part of the end-user documentation  of the software.

The IDE has created a new empty form. Now we're going to make some changes to it.

You have to have access to the **Object Inspector**. If it's not already on the screen, you can click on VIEW and pick Object Inspector. By Default, the Object Inspector will show details for the form itself, but later you will see that it shows and allows changes, to whatever object is clicked ( a button, a label, a radio button, etc ).

**Name**: The first thing to do is to change the Name of the Form. All of the properties in the Object Inspector are in alphabetical order, so scroll down till you see Name and change the value on the right side from "Form1" to "Calc". As soon as you click on any property other than **Name**, the Name of the form will be changed, and so will the **Caption** of the form. It turns out that the Caption automatically becomes the same as the form's Name.

**Color:** The next thing to do is change the color of the form. In the Object Inspector, scroll up to **Color**. If you move your cursor over the far right end of that property line, a button with three dots appears ( those three-dots are called an elllipsis ). Pick a color. My favorite is yellow or some shade of blue.

**Width:** you should change the width of your form to 260. I think that is the number of pixels. By default, the form is just a little too wide for this project.

You could Compile/Link/and Run right now by clicking on the

green arrow it doesn't do much yet. ( the green GO arrow is the third icon from the left, on the second row from the top ).

It should compile and link with no errors, then run your app. Don't forget, you can stop your form from running, click on the standard **X** icon, to tell it to stop.

**Save Your Work:** Okay, in some ways I'm a creature of habit. When I start a new program, I tend to make a folder or sub-directory for the new program then use the basic names of the given language to save files. Let me show you how I save this program: I make a sub-directory called calc, now the first time I save, I press the "save all" icon. I navigate to the folder that I have made ( called calc ) the computer asks me for an .lpi name, but suggests project1.lpi, I clicked on save to accept that name. Now it asks me to save the .pas file and suggests unit1.pas ( in the new folder ) and I clicked on the save button to accept that name. If I want to back up the project, I just grab the \calc subdirectory and all of the files in there and drag them to my backup device. ( I really like to put them on a flash drive or my dropbox cloud account and then work on the project from there, but that doesn't always work ).

You can stop any Lazarus program that you have created and are running by clicking on the X button ( the upper right for Windows, and upper left for Linux and Apple ).

By default, the next time you start Lazarus, your last

project will be loaded automatically. If it doesn't load automatically, usually you can run the project menu ( top level Lazarus menu ), then open the menu choice **project.** Navigate to your folder and click on your project ( for me, it's usually project1.lpi ). On a couple of occasions, with a Linux machine, I had to restart the computer to get my program to load correctly.

Now's a good time to add a copyright notice at the top of your program source. In the source editor, go all the way to the top where you will see "Unit unit1;". You can make a new line above that and enter:

{ (c) copyright 2014 James Booth}

Put in your name, not mine, and the current year. Anything between the squiggly brackets is a comment and will not be processed by the compiler. Any work written in America after 1977 is automatically covered by American copyright law, even without a copyright notice. Your attorney will be glad you put your name in the source because it's a crime, in the US, to remove it, so it kind of says "this is mine", and "I mean it."

Now if you plan to use any of the popular Open Source licenses for your project. You can click on "Source" in the Top menu then highlight "Insert General", you can then pick from any of the popular open source licenses, most of them are listed there. You usually have to put in the year and your name, or your company's name. If you are producing a commercial program. You should probably enter the phrase "All Rights

Reserved" under or by your name as part of your copyright notice. Just like the one at the beginnig of this book.

**Global variables:** Scroll down in the source code editor until you see the word "implementation" and just above it, you will see var and just below that, calc: tcalc; below that you can put in your description of your global variables. Pascal is a strongly typed language. Programmers usually frown upon the use of global variables, but in this case ( a small app ) their use makes pretty good sense  I'll put in a couple of global variables that I'm sure we'll need, it will look something like this:

```
var
   calc:tcalc;
   s:string;
   r,r1,r2:real;
   pt:boolean;
   func:char;
```

I'm sure we'll come back to this later....

 **Here's something you'll want to know**: When our program first launches the form we can have a program run automatically. OnCreate or OnActivate are good places to put code that we want to run at the beginning of the program. Here's how: In the Object Inspector, click on the Events tab ( while our form, calc, is highlighted ) Now that the Events tab is highlighted, double click in the empty space to the right of the word OnActivate. The made-up word "FormActivate" will appear. The neat part is that

Lazarus will create the skeleton of the procedure.

```
procedure          Tcalc.FormActivate(Sender          Tobject);
begin

end;
```

This new procedure appears in the source editor. A method ( if you use object oriented languages we use the word method ) for the form calc. Any code that you put between the begin and end pair will run as soon as the form is activated ( just about as soon as it appears ). I use this procedure to initialize my global variables.

To move this project to another PC, you should transfer six files to the new PC regardless of the Operating System, these files are:

project1.LPR
project1.LPI
project1.LPS
project1.RES
unit1.FRM
unit1.PAS

Put these six files in a sub-directory ( or folder ) and then load them as a project from the top menu of Lazarus. Once loaded as a project, you can compile, link and run the transferred program on the new machine.

 I've had the best experience when the target machine is running Windows. I'm not saying that there is anything wrong with the non-Windows versions of Lazarus, but the Windows version may have a little more polish since Microsoft Windows users are likely the largest user base for the Lazarus IDE as of now.

Our calculator form looks like this now:

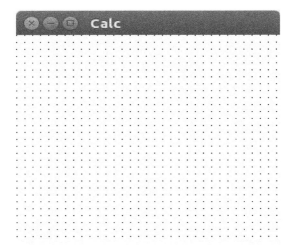

# Chapter 2

In this chapter, we're going to populate our form with several controls that are required by our calculator project.

---

- EditBox

- Keypad Buttons

- Learn how Align Works

- Object Names

- OnClick – What's That About?

---

First, we need to have a display, just like any calculator. For this we will use a standard **editbox.** To put one on your form just click on the editbox icon ( The icon for the editbox is the fifth one from the left while the standard tab is chosen ). Click where you want the upper left of your editbox, then drag the box to its lower right of your editbox. It will take up most of the width of your form. We are going to make some changes to our editbox.

Change the editbox. Here's how: Look at your Object Inspector, find your new editbox, its called Edit1:Tedit. In the Object Inspector, click on Edit1:Tedit in the upper-left panel of the Object Inspector. We are going to change three things about the edit box. Find Alignment and move to the property panel ( the right-hand side ) and click the box ( with the down-pointing arrow ) at the end of the line and pick taRightJustify. This causes things printed in our editbox to appear right justified ( I'll bet you guessed that ). Lets change the font, if you scroll down a bit to the font property, click on the box at the right end of the line and pick a font for your editbox. I used a mono-spaced font ( every number is the same width ) – my favorite is called Aaargh of about 14 points. Now, we're going to find the Name ( properties are in alphabetical order ) change it to "dis" ( short for display ). Last, we'll change the text ( the default text is Edit1 ) to a space ( or a blank ), the character for blank. Simply find "Text" in the object inspector and change the value to ' '.

While this program only needs one form, it needs a bunch of buttons ( after all, it is a calculator ). Now we'll be putting on a keypad. This is where my form and yours may differ. The fonts that you use might look different than mine, but don't worry. Remember, this is just an exercise for us to learn about Lazarus and Object Pascal.

**Now, a keypad.** Usually, we only need eleven buttons for a decimal keypad, zero through 9 and a decimal point. For this exercise, I'm going to make buttons with width and height of 22. I'll start by making three buttons that will eventually be 7, 8, and 9. For each button, the standard control tab of Lazarus should be chosen ( near the top of the screen ), click on the *button* icon, it should be the 4th icon from the left, the icon looks like a button that says OK on it. Now put the button on your form. Click the button icon. On your form, click on the upper left corner of where you want your button to be, drag to the lower right, of where your button will be and let the mouse button up. Go in the Object Inspector and make these changes to your button. Set the Height to 22 and set the Width to 22.

I'll bet you're wondering how I got these three buttons to line up together.

**Align:** Put your buttons on the form and then size them

( height & width ) then highlight all three of them. By using your mouse and pretending to draw a box around all three of your buttons, that will highlight them. Put your cursor on any of the buttons and right-click your mouse. Pick Align from the menu. Choose the radio button(s) that you need. Notice that buttons for Horizontal changes are on the left, and vertical change buttons are on the right. You will choose the best radio buttons depending what your buttons need to get them to be aligned. Play with the Align feature, you may find it to be a big time saver as I have. I picked the "Space equally" choice from the Horizontal list. Looks great.

**Lined up lines:** you will notice that when two objects or more are "lined up" horizontally or vertically on a form, Lazarus quickly displays a blue line between them to show that they are lined up. This turns out to be a very valuable feature for me,

Put in the rest of your buttons, till there are four rows of three each. I did it the easy way. I drew a box around my first three buttons to highlight them, then I right-clicked on one of them, and I chose "copy" from the list of choices. I move the 3 buttons down to the 4, 5, 6 position. I moved the cursor to a lower unused position, right-clicked the mouse and picked "paste". The first three buttons reappeared. Not in the exactly the right place, but 3 buttons together, I dragged them where I wanted them. Every time I right-clicked the mouse, and clicked paste, three more buttons appeared. Another row of buttons. I did it until I had four rows of buttons. The rows will start with 7, 4, 1, 0. Its a keypad!

Now we have a bunch of buttons, but they don't do anything yet.

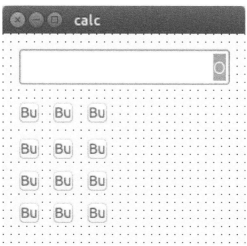

When you create a new button, Lazarus gives it a **name**, like Button14. Just in case you forget to. No two objects can have the same **name** because Lazarus tracks all of it's objects by name. When you give your object a name, Lazarus takes care of most of the changes for you – you'll see.

We're going to rename each of our buttons and put a character in the button's caption ( which shows up on the face of the button ).

**Name & Caption:** Go to your top most, left most button. This will become button seven. Highlight that button on your form, then look over at your Object Inspector and scroll down to Name. It will probably have a value of "Button1", drag over that name, and type in "seven", the new Name. Scroll up to **Caption** and change it to "7", the numeral seven character. After you click just about any place else( on any other property ), the new Caption appears on the button. Now, do

25

the same with Button2, so it will have the Name "eight" and the Caption of "8". Let's do the same with the rest of our buttons. Four, five, six, one, two, three.

WAIT, when you get to zero you will need a decimal point too ( mostly for decimal math ). If we want to, we could remove the extra button ( between zero and the decimal point ) and make the zero wider. That's what I did.

**OnClick :** To make your calculator work, with the left button of your mouse, you click to press the buttons on the keypad and for each press, you get a number on the display line. We'll make that work with our program here. I'll show you how.

In any GUI program, when the user clicks a button, the computer jumps to a piece of code that handles the key that has been pressed. In Lazarus, key presses, are handled by procedures.

Let's see how it works:

While your form is not running, go visit your '7' button, click on it in the form, to highlight it. In the Object Inspector, you should see the properties for your '7' button - named 'seven'. Click on the Events tab in the Object Inspector. Locate the 'OnClick' event. In the empty space on the line to the right, if you double-click, a new Procedure will be created in the source editor called 'sevenClick'. Lazarus will put in the procedure declaration and the begin and end statements – it will even put your cursor right where it needs to be for you to write some new handler pascal code.

Lazarus writes the following code for you:

```
procedure Tcalc.sevenClick(Sender: TObject);
begin

end;
```

Between the begin and end we write the code that we want to run when the user clicks the button. For now, we need just a couple of lines.

```
s:=s+'7';
dis.text:=s;
```

The first line of code tells the computer that the value displayed by should be 's' ( a string ) with the character '7' appended to the right end of it. 'Dis' is the name of our one and only display line. Any strings assigned to dis.text are displayed in our little calculator display instantly. The second line tells the computer to display our updated string ( 's' ).

Our OnClick button click handling procedure in the source editor looks like this now:

```
procedure Tcalc.sevenClick(Sender: Tobject);
begin

  s:=s+'7';
  dis.Text:=s;
end;
```

Let's do the same work with our '8' button. Find the button, highlight it, in the Object Inspector, click on the Events tab and double-click on the value area of OnClick event. Put s:=s+'8'; and dis.text:=s; in the eightClick procedure, in the source editor.

Between the begin and end. Put in the source with the proper number character ( depending on the key your are editing ) Let's do it for all our keys. You'll speed things up if you use copy and paste.

# Chapter 3

- Clear & Back-Space

- Checking the input

- Boolean – what's that? How to use the IF statement.

- ShowMessage – How to make that work

I'm looking at a calculator ( a Cannon brand ) on my desk. Near the top of calculator there are two buttons that are red ( most buttons are some shade of gray ). The red buttons are C for clear and CE for clear-error. We're going to put similar buttons on our calculator.

I put my clear and backspace buttons on the same hoizontal line as my 7,8, and 9 buttons.. First I put both buttons on the form. Then I changed their names to **clear** and **backspace**. I made a new OnClick key-press handler by highlighting the appropriate button ( I did clear first ), highlighted the event tab and double-clicked on value area of the OnClick event. I used the OnClick event of the clear button to blank the 's' string.

```
s:='';
```

Since we are working with a real computer instead of a calculator's CE key, a clear-error key, we can have an actual backspace key. It's so simple. We just strip the last character off our display string. Here's how to do it:

```
l:=length(s);
s:=copy(s,1,l-1);
dis.Text:=s;
```

First, we get the current length of our display string 's' and place it in an integer variable l ( really short for 'length' ). Next, we use 'Copy' ( a Pascal command ) to get the sub-string of the 's' string starting at index 1 going to the length minus 1 character. You see, an object pascal string is really just a built-in single dimensional array of characters with maximum length of 256. The s:=copy(s,1,l-1); means the string 's'' should have the value of the old version of 's', but not the whole string. Instead we get the string starting at character 1, all the way to the end less one character. It appears to 'back up' one character each time you click the BS key.

We don't have much to worry about when it comes to **checking the input**, since the user can only enter the characters from the keypad, and we control those. The only way that the user's number can vary is a number can only have a single decimal point. Easy. In the global variables, I added a shortened version of point called pt. It is **boolean**, so it can only have the values of true or false. By default, **pt is false** which means there is no decimal point in the current number. The first time a user puts in a decimal point, the boolean variable pt is set to true. If the user tries to enter a second decimal point, not only does the point not appear, but a message telling the user that a second decimal point is not allowed. We use the **IF statement** to test pt so the computer knows what to do.

The message appears using a built-in procedure that can be called with a single line of code. Here's how we do it:

When the user clicks on the point button, the computer will jump to the pointClick handler procedure and the first thing it does is to test if pt is false ( a decimal is not in the number if pt is false ). Pt is a "sort-of" flag. If pt is still false, then a point is appended to our 's' string and pt is set to true ( there is now a decimal point in our number ).

If pt is true, the number cannot accept another decimal point. Instead, we send a message to the user with the **ShowMessage** command. In it's simplest form it looks like this:
ShowMessage('sorry, this number can have'

+#13#10+'only one decimal point.');

The plus sign means append or add this to the earlier string. The #13 and #10 are codes left over from the early days of PCs and really mean, "include a carriage return and line feed because this is a two line message". It says "you can only put one point in this number". The message will pop up in the middle of the screen in it's own box, and will require the user to click on the OK button to continue.

# Chapter 4

We're coming to the end of this exercise where we we will soon have a complete working calculator. In this chapter we will add the 'function' buttons and learn how to make them work. With the completion of this chapter we will have built our working calculator!

- Function buttons – codes

- the Case Statement

- Color of Buttons (doesn't work in Windows)

- Clean up our form

Now we're ready to make our project into a real calculator – make it calculate. To do that, we have to have *function* keys. You know, make it add and subtract and such. The first thing to do is to put our arithmetic function buttons on our form.

You should put on one button each for the functions addition, subtraction, multiplication, and division. You can see in the diagrams on these pages that I made my calculator look similar to my desktop unit. I made the plus key taller but all the keys are the same width. I lined up the multiplication key and the addition key under 'Clear' and the division, subtraction and equals key under the back-space key. You might want to do the same. Just make sure they all get on the form, then we can tell them what to do.

If you say, out loud, what you want your calculator to do, it will be pretty obvious what your program must do. So "ten plus five...and it equals...". You can hear that each time we say a function like 'plus', we have one number and we are about to say another. We say ten, we need to save that, - then 'plus', our function, - five, our next number, - then equals, - then display the answer.

Knowing this, as soon as a function key is pressed, we should save the current value ( held in dis.text remember, our displayed value ), convert it to a real number and store it in n1. We've created two variables to hold our numbers to be acted on ( added, multiplied, divided or subtracted ) and we're going to store the first one in n1. We want to make note of the function key pressed so **we are going to assign a 'function letter' code to a character variable named 'func'**. ( 'p' for plus, 'm' for multiply, 's' for subtract and 'd' for divide ) I know, I'm not very creative.

This is good though. By assigning a single character to the func variable, we can use a **Case Statement** to make our calculator work. You see, the Case statement works with characters and integers, but not strings. It's easy to set up and usually faster than if statements. Look at the code. It should be plain to see. The Case Statement figures out what to do based on the 'func' code ( p, m, s, or d)

Our equals button is a good way to get our calculator to calculate. "Ten plus five" *equals.* Well, we put 10 in n1 and then 5 in n2. In this example we have set the function code in the plus button handler to 'p' for *plus* – addition so in our case statement, we add n1 and n2 and we put the answer ( 15 ) in the real-type variable 'n'. The user is expecting to see the answer in the display so I've told the computer to convert the answer to a string, then place it in dis.text.

The programming looks like this:

```
begin
        plus.Color:=clDefault;
        n2:=strtofloat(s);
        n:=n1+n2;
        s:=floattostr(n);
        dis.text:=s;
end;
```

I did one other thing – I changed the **color of the 'plus' button** to a sky blue when the user clicked the function key. When the user clicks the equal key, the button is set back to the clDefault color which is some shade of gray. I don't think this color thing works in the Windows version of Object Pascal, and from my research, it probably won't be fixed. It works fine on Ubuntu Linux.

We need to copy a series of commands ( from the previous page – the entire block of code - the begin, end and everything in between ), and paste it in for the three other functions ( m, s, and d ) in the case statement. Don't forget to change the operator to the correct one ( *,-,/) So that n1 and n2 are multiplied, subtracted or divided to give the correct results. My working source code is on the following pages so you can see what I did. There is only one Case Statement in the code, so it should be easy to find.

Hard to believe but true: we have a working four function calculator. Go ahead and run it – it should work. If it doesn't work, you did something wrong. Look at your source code and see if you can find the problem. If you have to, look at my code for a hint. It's not cheating, that's why you bought the book!

**Clean up the form:** I did do another thing, I narrowed the display window and changed the width of the form to  195. I also shrunk the height down to 200. This makes the calculator easier to fit in a corner of the screen. Like any other tool, you can drag it around by clicking and holding on the title-bar and drag it anywhere you want it. For all intents and purposes we're done. I have a few interesting bits in the thoughts chapter and the source code chapter might be valuable to some of you. This is what my calculator looked like when it was done.

# Chapter 5

Thoughts

---

* adding features

* smaller executables

---

This book was written to get you through just the calculator. There is so much more to learn. Me and you, we're just learning but there are people who know this stuff forward and backward. They know how the language (Free Pascal) works and the details of the Lazarus IDE and how it does things. I see them doing amazing things – you can check some of them out at www.lazarus.freepascal.org

While you were finishing up your calculator, you were probably thinking of ways you could **add features** to our project. Me too!

Multiple bases. I know that I could use other bases myself so I added that feature to my calculator. I put binary, base 2, and octal, base 8 as well as hexadecimal, base 16. Why those? Those bases are used in various computers. I added a radio group and a radio button for each base. You could type in a number in base 10 ( that's what we all learned in second grade – that's what our calculator uses now ) then click my base 16 button and the number would be converted to base 16. To hurry the project along in my calculator, all the math is done in base 10. It just so happens that routines for Object Pascal to do all the base conversions already exist. You might also add a Pi key, and a square root key. You might also add the most trigonometric functions too. Pretty neat. Don't forget, you have to include keys A through F for hexadecimal.

On-screen paper tape. This feature would 'remember' each transaction the user enters, then the computer displays them on the screen, in a special section of our form. When the next transaction is entered, the previous transaction is moved up the screen and the last one is displayed at the bottom. I never implemented this feature, but I thought about it a lot.

Memory functions. This allows the user to save a number for later use. Usually you would have a M+ key and sometimes a M-key, a memory recall key, MR, and almost always a MC key for clearing the value in memory. ( Yah, I put this feature in my calculator ). The M+ key adds the displayed number to the single memory register, where the M- key subtracts the current value from the memory amount. The MR, memory recall button, brings up the number in memory on the display so the user can use it in a transaction.

Active parentheses. If I had this, I could use parenthesis to do more complex math problems. When I thought about this I looked through my stuff and found a program I had previously written that did some of this. My old program was written in Algol ( I had almost no idea what machine I had written the parenthesis program on because Algol has been around since before I was born and is still around today ). I decided not to use the old program because I didn't remember exactly how it worked. It was poorly commented ( yep, I wrote it ) and I noticed that there was some recursion in the old routine. I don't like recursion on a PC or a phone because you can run out of memory unexpectedly.

I decided not to add any other features because it would make the book too long and the program too long. People get tired. If the lesson is too long, programmers get bored and they quit.

You may have noticed that your calculator executable is really big. Mine is 21.7MB. Ouch! It's so big because there is bunch of debugging information embedded by the Lazarus IDE, the compiler and the linker. You can **shrink the executable**. Just go to the Project menu choice and click on the 'Project options' menu choice. Now click on 'compiler options'. Over on the left about two/thirds of the way down you will see Linking. Click on Linking. Now, un-check every box and check the box next to 'Strip symbols from executable ( -Xs )'

Now when you recompile and relink your application, it will be much smaller. My calc is only 4.4 megabytes now. The smaller application loads much faster .

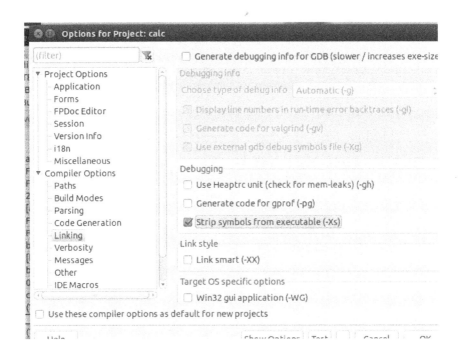

# Chapter 6

Here is my complete source code for the calc project

```
{ (c) copyright James Booth }
{   All Rights Reserved        }
unit Unit1;

{$mode objfpc}{$H+}

interface

uses
    Classes, SysUtils, FileUtil, Forms, Controls, Graphics, Dialogs,
StdCtrls;

type
  { Tcalc }

  Tcalc = class(TForm)
```

```
    multiply: TButton;
    divide: TButton;
    subtract: TButton;
    equal: TButton;
    plus: TButton;
    clear: TButton;
    backspace: TButton;
    seven: TButton;
    zero: TButton;
    point: TButton;
    eight: TButton;
    nine: TButton;
    four: TButton;
    five: TButton;
    six: TButton;
    one: TButton;
    two: TButton;
    three: TButton;
    dis: TEdit;
    procedure backspaceClick(Sender: TObject);
    procedure clearClick(Sender: TObject);
    procedure divideClick(Sender: TObject);
    procedure eightClick(Sender: TObject);
    procedure equalClick(Sender: TObject);
    procedure fiveClick(Sender: TObject);
    procedure FormActivate(Sender: TObject);
    procedure fourClick(Sender: TObject);
    procedure multiplyClick(Sender: TObject);
    procedure nineClick(Sender: TObject);
    procedure oneClick(Sender: TObject);
    procedure plusClick(Sender: TObject);
    procedure pointClick(Sender: TObject);
    procedure quitCalick(Sender: TObject);
    procedure sevenClick(Sender: TObject);
    procedure sixClick(Sender: TObject);
    procedure subtractClick(Sender: TObject);
    procedure threeClick(Sender: TObject);
    procedure twoClick(Sender: TObject);
    procedure zeroClick(Sender: TObject);
  private
    { private declarations }
```

```pascal
public
  { public declarations }
end;

var
  calc: Tcalc;
  s,s2:string;
  l:integer;
  n,n1,n2:real;
  pt:boolean;
  func:char;
implementation

{$R *.lfm}

{ Tcalc }

procedure Tcalc.quitCalick(Sender: TObject);
begin
  application.Terminate;
end;

procedure Tcalc.sevenClick(Sender: TObject);
begin
  s:=s+'7';
  dis.Text:=s;
end;


procedure Tcalc.sixClick(Sender: TObject);
begin
  s:=s+'6';
  dis.Text:=s;
end;

procedure Tcalc.subtractClick(Sender: TObject);
begin
  n1:=strtofloat(s);
  s:=''; dis.text:=s;
  func:='s';
  subtract.Color:=clSkyBlue;
```

```
  pt:=false;
end;

procedure Tcalc.threeClick(Sender: TObject);
begin
  s:=s+'3';
  dis.Text:=s;
end;

procedure Tcalc.twoClick(Sender: TObject);
begin
  s:=s+'2';
  dis.Text:=s;
end;

procedure Tcalc.FormActivate(Sender: TObject);
begin
  s:='';
  pt:=false;
  n:=0;
  n1:=0;
  n2:=0;
  func:=' ';
end;

procedure Tcalc.fiveClick(Sender: TObject);
begin
  s:=s+'5';
  dis.Text:=s;
end;

procedure Tcalc.eightClick(Sender: TObject);
begin
  s:=s+'8';
  dis.Text:=s;
end;

procedure Tcalc.equalClick(Sender: TObject);
begin
  case func of
```

```
'p'  :begin
        plus.Color:=clDefault;
        n2:=strtofloat(s);
        n:=n1+n2;
        s:=floattostr(n);
        dis.text:=s;
      end;
'm'  :begin
        multiply.Color:=clDefault;
        n2:=strtofloat(s);
        n:=n1*n2;
        s:=floattostr(n);
        dis.text:=s;
      end;
's'  :begin
        subtract.Color:=clDefault;
        n2:=strtofloat(s);
        n:=n1-n2;
        s:=floattostr(n);
        dis.text:=s;           end;
'd'  :begin
        divide.Color:=clDefault;
        n2:=strtofloat(s);
        n:=n1/n2;
        s:=floattostr(n);
        dis.text:=s;
      end;
  end;
end;

procedure Tcalc.clearClick(Sender: TObject);
begin
  pt:=false;
  s:='';
  n1:=o;
  n2:=o;
  dis.text:=s;
  func:=' ';
  plus.Color:=clDefault;
  subtract.Color:=clDefault;
  multiply.Color:=clDefault;
```

```
  divide.Color:=clDefault;
end;

procedure Tcalc.divideClick(Sender: TObject);
begin
  n1:=strtofloat(s);
  s:=''; dis.text:=s;
  func:='d';
  divide.Color:=clSkyBlue;
  pt:=false;
end;

procedure Tcalc.backspaceClick(Sender: TObject);
begin
  l:=length(s);
  s:=copy(s,1,l-1);
  dis.Text:=s;
end;

procedure Tcalc.fourClick(Sender: TObject);
begin
  s:=s+'4';
  dis.Text:=s;
end;

procedure Tcalc.multiplyClick(Sender: TObject);
begin
  n1:=strtofloat(s);
  s:=''; dis.text:=s;
  func:='m';
  multiply.Color:=clSkyBlue;
  pt:=false;
end;

procedure Tcalc.nineClick(Sender: TObject);
begin
  s:=s+'9';
  dis.Text:=s;
end;

procedure Tcalc.oneClick(Sender: TObject);
```

```
begin
  s:=s+'1';
  dis.Text:=s;
end;

procedure Tcalc.plusClick(Sender: TObject);
begin
  n1:=strtofloat(s);
  s:=''; dis.text:=s;
  func:='p';
  plus.Color:=clSkyBlue;
  pt:=false;
end;

procedure Tcalc.pointClick(Sender: TObject);
begin
  if pt=false then begin
                   s:=s+'.';
                   dis.Text:=s;
                   pt:=true;
              end
         else
                   ShowMessage('sorry, this number can have'
                      +#13#10+'only one decimal point.');


end;

procedure Tcalc.zeroClick(Sender: TObject);
begin
  s:=s+'0';
  dis.Text:=s;
end;

end.
```